RETIREMENT
MADE
SIMPLE

(yes, really.)

DAVID M RAGLAND

© 2018 RETIREMENT MADE SIMPLE | DAVID M RAGLAND

ISBN 978-1-946978-82-0

TABLE OF CONTENTS

Author's Introduction

Race Day

The obnoxious buzzing in my ear at 3:45 a.m. is a relief. I've slept fitfully all night while trying to ignore the uneasiness in my stomach. I am restless, nursing a stomach full of nerves.

I quickly dress and head to the kitchen, although the thought of eating breakfast triggers a wave of nausea. I feel as if I'm on a boat in high seas, trying not to hurl over the rail. There is no way that I can skip breakfast because my body needs the energy, a lot of energy. I gulp down a protein shake in one continuous swallow followed by two hard-boiled eggs. Now I really feel as if I will be sick.

From the edge of the kitchen, I hear my coach's voice, "Just relax. Stay calm. Stick to the plan." I look at him as he calmly sips his coffee. My first thought is "that's easy for you to say, you're not about to jump into a human washing machine." As if reading my mind, a Cheshire cat grin spreads across his face. "You're the one who wants this," he says. I feel sick all over.

My brother and a friend are ready and waiting. "Show time," one says, yawning. Now the wave of panic hits. Do I have everything? Where are my goggles? I sift through my bags and check the bedroom dresser; berating myself for not having an extra pair. I'm going to be late because of a $10 pair of goggles. Finally, I find them at the bottom of my gear bag.

The sky is pitch black as we arrive at the race start. Headlamp-wearing volunteers direct traffic, people and equipment. Huge portable lights illuminate the area as generators hum in the background. There's a surreal calm despite the thousands of people gathering. As we unload, I do a final check: wet suit, gear bags, special needs bags.

A nervous energy permeates the area where the volunteers apply body markings with massive black felt-tip markers that remind me of Obi-Wan Kenobi and his light saber. We all make chit-chat while waiting for our race numbers to be painted on our upper arms and our age on the back of our left calves.

In every race, the numbers are different. Once the markings are on, that's when I realize that "this is for real." Every race is a mix of first-timers and elite pros and you can always feel the shared emotions. The only thing I can do is remind myself that I've prepared and that I have a plan.

I meld into a sea of humanity while heading towards the swim start and the thousands of other wetsuit-clad competitors.

Through the crisp, clear air, the colors of the early morning sun reflect off the water. All I see is how cold it looks.

I bounce up and down on the balls of my feet hoping to keep my muscles warm and to stop the shivering. I rub my palms together and bring them to my mouth for a blast of warm air. My hands are clammy. This is my 22nd Ironman and my palms are still clammy on race day and I still feel like I'm about to throw up.

I take deep breaths and keep stretching. I mentally review the route and envision the pace while reminding myself that the unexpected will happen and I can't do anything about it. I know that I am well prepared and that I can get through anything the race throws at me.

The blast of the start gun cracks in the still morning air and in an instant, I'm sprinting, splashing and ultimately diving into the cold water with 3,000 others. The Ironman begins!

You don't have to be training for an Ironman to understand the emotional challenge that comes with starting something daunting and important. Are you facing your own start line? That line in the not too distant future where you will no longer be working but free to pursue your new life in retirement. Is your anticipation of your new life coupled with the fear of the financial and emotional unknown? Let us, together, prepare a simple plan to your retirement success and financial freedom.

CHAPTER ONE

YOU CAN

Beginning to Plan for Retirement

When I began training for the Ironman in 1996, my goal was simply to lose weight. My quest began with a photograph snapped during the Atlanta Olympics. In that photo, I saw the couch potato I'd become. I was more than 75 pounds above my college weight and I needed help. I wanted to get into shape and my ultimate goal became living a healthy lifestyle.

When I started my quest, I was scared. The thought of swimming 2.4 miles, riding 112 miles and running 26.2 miles was overwhelming. Back then only those "crazy" extremists would think of toeing the start line. We were training and racing by the seat of our pants. What were our training plans or race plans?

Today, Ironman racers come from all walks of life. Racers are tall, short, young, old, thin and large. These variations are a good thing. The explosion of information available through the Internet and Triathlon Coaches have made possible for many what once seemed impossible. We no longer race blindfolded throwing darts against a wall, but rather have defined training and racing plans to help guide us along the way. Today, anyone who is mentally prepared and is willing to put in the training time can complete an Ironman.

The race is simple. If you commit to the training then you will finish the race. The process is simple but not at all easy. Both discipline and consistency are required to do the work to complete the training. Many Ironman finishers will tell you that the race is the easy part once you've mastered the training.

Beginning to plan for retirement can seem as overwhelming as training for an Ironman. At first, the process can seem complicated. For many people, the process of retirement planning seems daunting and makes it difficult to balance your current wants and needs with your dreams for the future. Recent statistics reflect how many people are struggling to prepare for retirement.

> The average retirement lasts 18 years, during which the average Social Security retirement benefit is only $1,315 per month or $15,780 per year;

> One out of three Americans has no additional retirement savings to supplement their Social Security income; and

> As of 2017, the average total retirement
  savings is only $95,776.

The lack of savings can be directly attributable to the following three reasons:

> **Behavioral:** The emotional satisfaction of immediate gratification vs. the long-term benefit of saving coupled with a propensity toward procrastination.

> **Educational:** The lack of basic understanding of money including the benefits of the power of compound savings, pre-tax savings and asset allocation.

> **Fundamental:** The elimination or reduction of pension plan benefits for American workers and the rise of employee directed 401(k) plans.

Given these statistics and the causes behind them, it becomes clear that achieving financial security without a plan will result in a longer and more difficult road to retirement. With the help of a coach, anyone can achieve his or her financial goals. The first simple step toward a comfortable retirement is acknowledging the need for a plan. This plan will help to guide your decisions along the way.

You will have to make choices just as I do when the alarm clock goes off at 4:00 a.m. I have to make a choice to stay in bed or to head to the pool. After 22 Ironman seasons, getting up those mornings that I have scheduled to swim is still hard to do. Yet every time I finish a swim, I feel so refreshed and alive!

Just remember. When you plan, you achieve.

KEY TAKE-AWAYS:

> A COMFORTABLE RETIREMENT STARTS WITH A PLAN

> YOU HAVE TO CHOOSE TO START

THE FIRST SIMPLE
STEP TOWARD A
COMFORTABLE
RETIREMENT IS
ACKNOWLEDGING
THE NEED FOR
A PLAN.

CHAPTER TWO

✳ THE FINISH LINE ✳

Start with the End in Mind

The finish line at an Ironman is a magical place.

The thought of the finish line brings a lump in my throat and a tear to my eye. The culmination of so much hard work brings incredible joy to those who finish. Family members and friends who have lived and breathed the early morning swims, the long bike rides and the sacrificed hours required to get across that line feel that joy too. Everyone who finishes has their own personal reason why that finish line is so important to them.

When I saw the photo of me at the 1996 Olympic games, I was shocked. That's not me, I screamed inside. I still saw myself as the lean guy who just graduated from college. When I looked in the mirror each day, I did not notice what was going on. The weight gain was happening so slowly. Day after day, week after week, I became just a little heavier. I did not notice until I saw that photo. Admitting a problem and doing something about it are two different things. Knowing that I was overweight was one thing, but doing something about it was another. I needed something to inspire me to set new goals.

Almost six months later, I was watching a television broadcast of the 1996 Ironman and was amazed that any one individual could ever complete such a race. I watched in sheer amazement when I saw a father and son doing the race together. The Ironman race is not a team sport but this father and son duo was no ordinary team. Due to a birth defect, the son was diagnosed as a spastic quadriplegic with cerebral palsy. The father literally swam while pulling his son in a life raft for 2.4 miles. He then rode a bike for 112 miles with the son on the front of the bike and then he pushed his son 26.2 miles in a wheel chair! After seeing that broadcast, I committed to getting back into shape; losing the weight and facing the demons that had resulted in my weight gain.

The Ironman finish line became my definitive goal. I knew that if I could cross the line I would lose the weight and I would change my life for the better. I saw the finish line not as the end, but as a new beginning. Do you have your own finish line in mind? Do you view retiring financially secure at the end of your work life as the finish line or as the start of something new?

Richard Branson was interviewed on CNBC and said, "I don't believe that retirement should be the goal." Just as finishing my first Ironman was my initial goal, the race simply became the first step towards a healthy and happy lifestyle.

In 2008, a survey was conducted by Transamerica and Gfk Roper Public Affairs and Media of more than 2,000 adults age 50 years or older. Out of their top 10 priorities in retirement, only two dealt with lifestyle choices. The majority (8 out of 10) of the surveyed priorities only dealt with the amount of money they had saved. However, lifestyle choices such as simplicity, flexibility and connectivity can be as important or more important than the actual amount of money you have in retirement. Is retiring financially secure your goal or just your starting point?

Saving for the future is understandably hard when 8 out of the 10 reasons to save represent a number on a piece of paper versus a clear picture of your future; something that you can emotionally grab onto. Being able to see the future emotionally provides the motivation you will need to make the right behavioral choices when it comes to saving versus spending.

Sports visualization has become one of the athletes' most powerful training tools. Seeing the perfect pitch or imagining the record setting downhill ski run can be as much of the success as the physical training of the human body. When you envision financial freedom or retirement, what does it actually look like in your mind? Would it be traveling, volunteering or golfing? Or is it even more than that?

When I envisioned financial freedom, I saw what was truly missing. Having enough money to live the life that I wanted and to live in a world where I made the decisions of how, when and where I was going to live my life. In a nutshell, what was really important to me was the ability to **choose**.

Is a financially secure retirement your goal? Could this simply be the first step to living a life free of worry that allows you to live the life you have always dreamed of? Should you begin today to "re-define" your top 10 priorities for retirement?

Defining and imagining goals with meaningful and measurable benchmarks helps you to clearly plan. Specific planning enables you to accomplish your goals and then provide for the emotional celebration of their attainment.

Key Take-Aways:

> Visualizing your goals makes them more attainable

> Lifestyle choices as well as financial targets are important

BEING ABLE TO
SEE THE FUTURE
EMOTIONALLY
PROVIDES THE
MOTIVATION TO
MAKE THE RIGHT
CHOICE WHEN IT
COMES TO SAVING.

CHAPTER THREE

TIME

Make Time Count

I have been fortunate to race in Ironman competitions in some of the most beautiful locations around the globe. Whether the race was in the South of France, Southern California or on the Big Island of Hawaii, I was always thrilled when the plane landed so that I could pursue the next finish line!

Be it either on a domestic or international flight, I am sure you have heard the announcement many times: "Please bring your seat backs and tray tables to their upright and locked positions as we will be landing shortly." Regardless if you are flying First Class, Economy Comfort or Coach, the rush of anticipation and the excitement of the next vacation comes over you. You are ready to be on the ground and get to your chosen destination!

Most people are blissfully unaware of all that goes on in the cockpit to maneuver the plane from 30,000 feet to a safe landing. Typically, pilots begin lining up the plane more than 60 miles out from the runway. Pilots check wind speed, weather at the airport, descent rate and a multitude of other factors to coordinate a successful landing. Timing the descent of the plane too fast results in huge amounts of fuel being wasted by flying the jet at a low altitude. Wait too long to descend, the plane can over shoot the landing zone and must circle the airport and delay the landing.

Just as the pilot is focused on an "on-time" arrival at the gate, the individual needs a timeline for which to build their financial plan. As you begin to clearly identify your retirement goals, your retirement date becomes your landing zone.

A fixed retirement date is one part of the time equation when designing a successful financial plan. Time can also be viewed as a period over which we perform specific tasks to accomplish financial goals as well as a tool we use to allow our assets to grow under the benefits of compound interest.

Let us look at each element of the time equation.

First, time as defined by a date in the future: Your retirement date simply creates a stake in the ground that holds you accountable for its completion. The specific date is a deadline to work towards. This date acts as the destination to measure progress against, letting you know if you are on-time, ahead of schedule or late to the gate!

Second, time as a timeline: By having a specific target date, we now have a period of time to accomplish our goals as well as a framework to help us make good long term financial decisions. For example, if our time line is 18 years and we are purchasing a new home with the goal to be debt free in retirement, then selecting a 30-year mortgage would not fit within our timeline and thus the purchase of a home must be affordable with a 15-year mortgage. The timeline can be used as a system to balance our purchases for today and saving for the future. The timeline, without shame or condemnation, provides immediate feedback on decisions to be made regarding a financial plan.

Third, time can be the most powerful asset in your journey to financial freedom with the benefits of compound interest. Simply put, the more time you have to save, the less money you will actually need to save in order to meet your financial goals. For example, if the goal is to have a $1.0 million-dollar nest egg in retirement, you would have to save the following amounts based upon the amount of time you have to save:

TIMELINE	MONTHLY SAVINGS	TOTAL SAVED	GOAL AMOUNT
10-year:	$5,778	$693,360	$1,000,000
20-year:	$1,920	$460,800	$1,000,000
30-year:	$820	$295,200	$1,000,000
40-year:	$381	$182,880	$1,000,000

Notice the difference for someone who started their savings 40 years before retirement versus those that started within 10 years of retirement. Time "adds" $306,640 to the amount of actual savings towards the $1.0 million-dollar nest egg over a ten-year period. On the other hand, time would "create" $817,120 of the $1.0 million-dollar nest egg over a 40-year period! More than 80% of the nest egg would be "free money" created by time.

Now we see why time is really an asset for all retirement savers and the more time you have to save, the better off you will be. Creating financial wealth is really about time and emotion. The more time you have, the less you need to save each month. The less you need to save each month will result in less "emotional" cost that you will have to spend. Saving more always requires the choice of not spending or of consuming less. Would it not be easier to save $381 per month than $5,778 per month? The process needs to be as easy as possible. The benefits of considering time as an asset of our planning include:

> More time to save

> More time for investments to grow

> More time to pay down debt

Beginning to save earlier is easier both emotionally and economically.

KEY TAKE-AWAYS:

> TIME IS AN ASSET

> START EARLY IN YOUR PLANNING AND INVESTING

TIME CAN BE THE MOST POWERFUL ASSET IN YOUR JOURNEY TO FINANCIAL FREEDOM.

CHAPTER FOUR

 # DNF

Position Yourself for Success

Did Not Finish: DNF

These are the three letters that any Ironman racer dreads seeing by their name after the race. The Ironman starts at 7:00 a.m. and you have until 12:00 midnight to finish.

Most Ironman athletes will tell you that at some point in every race they considered quitting. You ask yourself "why am I doing this? Why am I killing myself?" The only thing between quitting and finishing is the will of the competitor. Every athlete has to make the choice to take the next stroke, turn the pedal just one more time and put one foot in front of the other. Continuing the race is up to each athlete and how committed he or she is to the finish line.

I have started twenty-two Ironman races, and I have finished twenty-two Ironman races. In my years, I have experienced a freak windstorm that made the water so choppy 500 out of 2,000 competitors did not finish the swim. I have endured a torrential rainstorm, which dropped more than 5 inches of rain during the day. I have experienced bike mechanical failures, stomach issues, cramping, heat, and exhaustion. In every race, I absolutely felt like quitting.

I finished every race. Am I just strong or lucky? Actually, neither of the two.

When I began Ironman, I knew that I had a lot to learn about racing and about myself. Rather than seeing Ironman as a race, I saw it as a journey. I soon figured out that the only thing that I could control was me. Those other things like wind, heat, or being kicked in the face while in the swim were totally out of my control. I chose to focus on what was within my control.

Are you focusing on things you can control when it comes to your financial future? How much you spend, how much you save, your use of debt and your lifestyle are all within your control. Are you worried and focused on things totally out of your control such as the stock market, the promotion you did not get or what your friends and neighbors have?

The first step towards any successful finish is showing up to the starting line. As with anything new, beginning is always the hardest. We all feel intimidated. I know that feeling all too well. After twenty-two Ironman races, you would think that it would be easy for me to start a race. The exact opposite is true. Each time I start a race I always feel queasy!

Taking control of your spending is the first step towards financial freedom. With any new client, we begin by completing a Spending Plan review. The Spending Plan review is simply a non-judgmental assessment of what someone is currently spending each month compared to how much money is coming in after tax. Rather than thinking about it as a budget, look at it as the first step towards taking control of your finances.

Take some time to review the sample Spending Plan on the next page. First, notice the break down between the three major categories:

> Debt payments

> Non-discretionary expenses (e.g., utilities, groceries, automotive expenses, etc.)

> Discretionary expenses (e.g., gifts, donations, clothes, dining out, etc.)

After you complete the Spending Plan, ask yourself, "how much am I spending each month for debt payments?" Are you spending 20, 30 or even 40 percent of your income on debt payments? How would your life change if you had all of your debt paid off? Next, ask, "how much am I spending on non-discretionary expenses?" How much of these non-discretionary expenses could be reduced if I could change my lifestyle?

Sample Spending Plan

DEBT PAYMENTS (A)

Auto Loan(s)

Credit Card(s)

HELOC

Mortgage(s)

Student Loan(s)

Other

SUBTOTAL $

% DEBT (A÷D)

NON-DISCRETIONARY EXPENSES (B)

Automotive (fuel, maintenance)

Auto Insurance

Auto Taxes

Cable & Internet

Electric, Gas, Water

Groceries

Home Insurance

Medical Insurance

Other Expenses

Pet Care

Phone(s)

Real Estate Taxes

Umbrella Insurance

SUBTOTAL $

% NON-DISCRETIONARY EXPENSES (B÷D)

DISCRETIONARY EXPENSES (C)

Clothing

Dining Out

Education Costs

Entertainment

Gifts

Donations

Other Expenses

Other Insurance (life, long-term care)

Personal Care (hair, spa, etc.)

Shopping

Subscriptions

Travel

Other

SUBTOTAL $

% DISCRETIONARY EXPENSES (C÷D)

GRAND TOTAL (D) $

PERCENTAGE FROM A+B+C 100%

The starting point in the race is to be willing to step up to the line. It can be emotionally tough to sit down and complete a spending plan. All sorts of emotions around spending and saving surface when completing this task. Recognizing that it is not always easy but taking the first step is the most important thing you can do. After its completion, you will not only feel a sense of accomplishment from finishing the plan, but you will begin to educate yourself about your money. I always say that the more you know about your money, the better off you will be.

Focusing your financial plan on the simple things that you can control will prepare you to handle life's unforeseen bumps along the way. What happens on race day happens. The wind, the rain, the heat and the humidity are going to happen. I know that the more time I focus on what I can control, such as my training leading up to the race, the better my outcome will be.

KEY TAKE-AWAYS:

> REVIEW CURRENT SPENDING

> START TAKING CONTROL OF WHAT YOU SPEND

ARE YOU FOCUSING
ON THINGS YOU CAN
CONTROL WHEN IT
COMES TO YOUR
FINANCIAL FUTURE?

CHAPTER FIVE

✳ SIMPLE WORKS ✳

Fundamentals for Retirement Planning

Eat, Train, Sleep, Repeat. I see this on bumper stickers, water bottles and everywhere else on race day. There's a reason for this mantra. As plans go, this is one of the best. Simple plans get accomplished.

If you search online, you will find dozens of triathlon and race training program websites. *Six Months to Race-Ready. Couch to Sprint in 12 Weeks. 18-Week Half-Iron Distance Program.* Do this, do that. Each plan is more detailed and more complex than the other. On one site, I counted 55 free plans. Choosing a training program can be overwhelming, but you have to have one to finish an Ironman. The same is true for achieving your retirement goals. The complicated financial plans may seem impressive, but if they are overwhelming then they will be harder to accomplish.

Search online for financial freedom, wealth management or retirement planning and the advice is even more overwhelming. There are thousands of tools, surveys, forms and plans at your fingertips. For example, sites promote Financial Freedom, interactive courses to "Take the Mystery out of Retirement," and integrative programs for financial blueprints. Browsing through the pages and pages of options becomes another hurdle in taking the first step. Rather than becoming overwhelmed, let's identify the simple first steps to becoming financially free.

You already have a starting point with a spending plan, now let's establish some basic principles when beginning to plan for financial freedom:

1. Being able to retire or to be financially free requires more money coming in than going out.

2. The less money you have going out, the less money you require coming in.

3. You will always have more control over the amount of money going out than you will over the amount coming in.

From the beginning, "Eat, Train, Sleep, Repeat" has been my mantra. Why? Because complicated plans don't get done. Simple plans get you to the finish line. By focusing on what we can control, such as our spending, we can build a plan that provides the foundation for long-term financial security and flexibility.

KEY TAKE-AWAYS:

> SIMPLE PLANS GET ACCOMPLISHED

> MONEY IN MUST BE GREATER THAN MONEY OUT

COMPLICATED FINANCIAL PLANS MAY SEEM IMPRESSIVE BUT CAN BECOME OVERWHELMING AND HARDER TO ACCOMPLISH.

CHAPTER SIX

✳ Training vs. Racing Plans ✳

Planning for Retirement vs. Being in Retirement

When I first started training for Ironman, more than 20 years ago, the thought of having a training plan was not on my radar screen. My buddies and I just swam, biked, and ran as much as we could. The more volume the better, regardless of how it impacted our businesses, bodies, and relationships. More was always better and we simply raced as fast as we could to get to the finish line. Needless to say, I usually ended the race in pain and disappointment as I walked across the finish line. With the help of a coach, anyone can achieve his or her financial goals.

Several years later, I learned about training plans which focused on cycles of heavy volume, tempo work, speed work and rest times. As I started to train with a plan my racing times got faster. Still, it was painful at the end of each race.

A few years ago, I engaged a new coach to help me redefine my Ironman racing. I eagerly awaited our first official planning session for the upcoming Ironman season. I spent hours gathering data on prior training plans and race results so that I could be prepared for a detailed planning session.

As soon as we sat down, I immediately shared my opinion regarding my previous training plans and suggested changes for the New Year. To my surprise, his first question had little to do with training. He asked me how I wanted my Ironman day experience to go. Did I just want to go fast and suffer through another race? Would I rather be present in the moment and actually enjoy all the day had to offer? Did I want to be able to experience the swim, revel in the bike ride, run with a smile on my face and actually finish strong? He explained to me that there is a difference between training plans to get me to the start line and a race day plan which defines how I was actually going to race the day.

I had never thought about the details of race day and how I could build a training plan around the actual experience I wanted to have. Are you making the same mistake when planning for your retirement? There are thousands of financial planning books and plans to choose from to help you make better tactical decisions. Plans are available to address what type of loan, what type of credit card, how to invest for the best returns and every other financial decision you could need. However, before you can make those decisions you must clearly define the financial side of retirement and the emotional changes that will occur once you no longer work. You have to plan for no paycheck but also address the changes in your emotional risk profile, your status in the community and the fact that you may be spending significantly more time with your spouse or significant other.

The following is a plan intended to be a road map for developing your financial future in retirement. Everyone is unique so it is not a step-by-step guidebook but rather a planning methodology. I use this process with hundreds of people in all stages of life to create a plan for retirement. Use this methodology to create a plan tailored to your retirement dreams.

KEY TAKE-AWAYS:

> YOU NEED A PLAN TO GET YOU TO RETIREMENT

> YOU ALSO NEED A PLAN FOR HOW YOU WILL LIVE IN RETIREMENT

CHAPTER SEVEN

※ EXPERIENTIAL RACING ※

Understanding Your Emotions and Money

Over time I began to view the Ironman race more as an experience rather than something I had to complete as fast as possible. I began to understand that I would need to make changes in many aspects of my training and racing. From the start, my coach explained that for the race plan to work, I would have to be more flexible both in my training and in my mindset. Some of the changes would be easy to adopt while others would be more difficult.

In our everyday lives, we have all probably been told, at some point, that we need to be more flexible. Whether it's your friends extolling the benefits of yoga, your spouse wanting you to try new things, or your general attitude towards the "curve balls" thrown at you, being more flexible helps us to achieve better outcomes in life.

Given this new outlook towards flexibility, not only would I have to "retrain" my body for a different type of racing, but also my emotional outlook on race day. Instead of going as hard and as fast as possible on every workout, my coach was proposing a more "balanced" approach to training with a lot of workouts planned at a very slow pace. This retraining of my body, using body fat as a primary energy source, would allow me to race all day without the highs and lows of the day affecting me. In a nutshell, I had to become a lot more flexible in my approach to training which would prepare me for the ups and downs that invariably come on race day.

Just as in Ironman racing, having the ability to be flexible in retirement is the key to being successful. Flexibility in retirement is needed both from a financial standpoint as well as for your emotional well-being. Flexibility from a financial standpoint is illustrated using the following example:

If your total monthly budget in retirement is $5,000 and you have $4,000 or 80% in fixed expenses, your ability to reduce expenses due to market downturns or unexpected expenses is very limited. This limitation can cause emotional panic and fear of running out of money in retirement leading you to make bad decisions. If, however, if your fixed expense were only $2,000 or 40% of the total, your ability to temporarily reduce your monthly spending is increased thereby reducing the emotional stress related to changes in the economic landscape.

As you can see, your ability to be flexible when making these decisions is directly related to controlling your financial and emotional well-being. In other words, flexibility puts you in control of your life so that you may decide when and where you will spend your money.

Given that more than 50% of current retirees' biggest fear in retirement is running out of money, we must develop a retirement plan that allows for maximum control of the money we spend each month. To achieve this goal, we must minimize those fixed, non-discretionary, expenses spent each month as a percentage of the total monthly expenses. Examples would include debt payments, utility costs, real estate taxes and insurance costs. By minimizing the percentage of those fixed expenses each month, we can better prepare for the emotional and financial ups and downs that come in retirement.

Whether it be stock market swings or unexpected one-time expenses such as a home repair, your fixed expenses should be a relatively small percentage of your total expenses. When you have built in flexibility and experience an unexpected shortfall, you can then decide to spend less money in any one month or over a period of time to compensate. As I have learned doing financial counseling for more than 20 years, when we separate our money-making decisions from our emotions, we generally make better financial choices. I have a phrase that I use frequently with clients: "the further you keep your money from your emotions, the more money you will have." By identifying and managing emotions which may lead to impulsive financial decisions, you begin to consistently make better long-term financial decisions.

By changing the way I trained for Ironman, my body used less energy for every swim stroke, bike pedal turn and running step so that I was more prepared when I decided to use a spike of energy to climb that hill or finish strong in the race. Minimizing your fixed expenses gives you the option of spending more money on the variable experiences of life you want to enjoy in retirement. Whether it's the family trip to Italy, helping out with educational expenses for your grandchildren or just having peace of mind that you are in control of how and when you spend your money, low fixed expenses are the key to that flexibility.

KEY TAKE-AWAYS:

> FLEXIBILITY IS KEY TO LIVING WELL IN RETIREMENT

> KEEP YOUR MONEY AND EMOTIONS SEPARATE

THE FURTHER YOU KEEP YOUR MONEY FROM YOUR EMOTIONS, THE MORE MONEY YOU WILL HAVE.

MORTGAGE
2ND MORTGAGE
CREDIT CARD
CAR LOAN
NEW KITCHEN
BANK LOAN
DEBT
DEBT

CHAPTER EIGHT

✳ WEIGHT MANAGEMENT ✳

Acknowledging the Burden of Debt

How many times did I look in the mirror in those pre-Ironman days and not notice the extra pounds that I carried? Sure, the clothes were getting tighter and I was sometimes out of breath after sprinting to the departure gate, but I did not really notice the pounds that were slowly being added to my frame. It was only when I saw the photo of what I had become during the Atlanta Olympics that caused me to make a change.

When I started my quest, I was afraid. The thought of carrying an extra 75 pounds on my small frame while racing was unthinkable. The extra pounds were the result of over indulging in the past. Simply put, I had taken in more calories from food and alcohol than my body had burned. I literally was paying the price for decisions in my past. Are you weighed down by decisions that you have made in the past in the form of the amount of debt that you have today?

If you feel like all of your income goes to debt payments, you are not alone. In the past, retirees had little to no debt when entering retirement. Today, more than ever before, those who are either close to or in retirement have record levels of debt. If you feel like you are drowning in debt, you are not alone.

Given that our plan for retirement is ultimate flexibility coming from low fixed monthly expenses, we must first tackle the weight of debt we are carrying today.

For me, taking the weight off boiled down to a simple equation. I had to burn more calories each day then I consumed. Simple? Yes. Easy? Well, not all the time. Losing weight is simple in that we have to get our bodies burning more calories by exercising, increasing our metabolic rate, making good food choices and letting nature take its course. In theory, it was simple. But I needed some mental motivation to stay on the plan in those first few weeks. I pulled out the old college photos from 10 years earlier and used those as a reference point for where I wanted to be. We all can get to our goals as long as we have the mental motivation to get there!

The same is true when we meet clients to discuss their financial future. We first sit down and complete a current spending plan. We then divide the total monthly debt payments by the total after tax income. More often than not we hear a big "WOW" or "I cannot believe that my debt is such a large percentage of my income." When you completed your spending plan from Chapter Four, what was your debt percentage? How much are you actually spending on debt payments for purchases you made in the past? How does that compare to spending money on things that you can enjoy today?

The WOW factor of knowing how much you spend on debt is the first step to making the change.

The next step is letting yourself imagine what you would do if you did not have those debt payments. I remember when I was overloaded with debt, I needed something to motivate me to get out of debt. I promised myself that if I got out of debt, every three months I would go on vacation and spend an amount equal to one month's debt payments. I gave myself a tangible goal that I could hold on to when I was going through the tough emotional times of getting out of debt.

What is your motivation to begin a debt elimination plan? A vacation goal? Just the feeling of being free of that monthly payment? Create a specific goal or reward to help keep you motivated. When I started to lose weight, I just keep telling myself how much easier it was going to be to bike 112 miles and run 26.2 miles with 75 fewer pounds on my body. Are you ready to get started on reducing your debt? Yes, you can. Remember, you can do this!

Key Take-Aways:

> How much are spending on debt each month?

> Imagine a life without debt payments

> Create a reward to keep you motivated

IMAGINE WHAT
EXPERIENCES YOU
COULD HAVE EACH
MONTH IF YOU
DID NOT HAVE TO
MAKE YOUR DEBT
PAYMENTS?

DEBTS:
1.
2.
3.
4.
5.

CHAPTER NINE

⁎ DEBT DETAILS ⁎

Tactical Planning for Getting Out of Debt

Knowing that I needed to lose weight was one thing, but actually doing it was another. I knew that my weight loss plan needed two things in order to be successful. The plan had to be simple and something that I could do on a consistent basis—and yes, it had to taste good! Coincidentally, I was invited to a lunch and learn by a close friend. The speaker was a well-known trainer and nutritionist who had worked with dozens of Olympic athletics over the years with much success.

This nutritionist introduced me to the concept of having a morning protein shake for breakfast. He told me that the morning protein shake would change my life. It did. I loved the chocolate protein shake because it fit my plan. It was simple: Two scoops of protein powder, water, banana and flax seed oil. It was consistent: As a chocolate lover, I could drink the same thing every day and never tire of it.

The protein shake gave me other benefits as well. First, it allowed me to start every day in a positive way. Nutritionally I could start my day knowing that I was doing something good for my body. This protein shake also gave me a positive mental boost to know that I was moving towards my goal.

Given that I was doing the shake seven mornings a week, I was consuming more than 30 percent of my meals in a healthy way. I could usually eat something nutritious for lunch which now meant close to 70 percent of what went into my body was healthy! Since I was eating 70 percent of my meals in a healthy way, when I did have a "cheat" meal I did not beat myself up about it. Most diets fail because we feel deprived. The diet is too strict. In the end, we end up failing and gaining more weight than before. Creating a balanced approach to a diet plan by mostly eating good meals, with a few indulgences along the way, allowed me to stay on the plan for the long term. Whether you are trying to lose weight or reduce debt, it's a long road and we cannot feel as if we are totally deprived along the way.

Creating a debt reduction plan, in my opinion, is the same as losing weight. In order for you to stay on track, the plan must be simple and it must be one that you can stay on for the long term. The lure of a quick fix can be tempting, but it's important to recognize that a fast solution, be it weight loss or debt reduction, is rarely successful. One must emotionally accept that getting out of debt is a marathon and not a sprint. Having a balanced plan over time, allows one to enjoy the journey along the way.

Reducing debt comes down to two simple steps:

> Don't incur any new debt

> Pay down the debt a little bit every month

The first step starts with looking at your current spending plan. Am I being smart with my purchasing decisions? Do you have more money going out than coming in? A simple equation tells us that in order to reduce your debt, you must have more money coming in than going out. By separating outflows into three categories—debt payments, fixed non-discretionary expenses and discretionary variable expenses, we can clearly identify where the money is going. If you have more money coming in than going out, congratulations, you are on your way to being able to reduce your debt.

If you have more money going out than coming you may have to face the reality of making some changes. When trying to adjust spending, I first start by looking at all of my expenses and asking two questions:

> Can I reduce expenses and not really "feel" the change? I refer to these expenses as the necessary but negotiable expenses.

> What am I spending money on that does
not truly affect my quality of life?

Necessary, but negotiable expenses, are those that creep up on us all. These expenses include the cable bill, the insurance bills, the cell phone bills, and many others. These expenses alone don't seem like a lot but can add up each month. These bills are often ones that you can shop around for better pricing (i.e., spend less money for) but get roughly the same service.

The second category is the expenses that I spend money on that really don't affect my quality of life. You may need to ask yourself the following questions. Am I shopping at high-priced grocers rather than low cost options? Am I choosing to shop at retailers that cost more because I feel like I deserve to shop there? Am I letting company marketing influence what I buy, and thereby paying more for the same product at other retailers? Simply said, sometimes TJ Maxx works nearly as well as Neiman Marcus.

By reviewing your spending plan, you have the power to decide how you spend your money. Remember that this is a long-term plan and you must balance living for today with having enough money to get you out of debt over time. You control the amount of money you have left over to reduce your debt each month. Once you have examined your monthly outflows and have maximized the amount of money you have to reduce your debt, consider the following practical steps to reduce your debt with your available cash flow.

> **Organize your debt based upon interest rate.** Make a list, in descending order based upon interest rate, of all of your outstanding debt balances. Usually credit card debt will be the highest and mortgage debt will be the lowest. Remember to factor in the tax deductibility of the mortgage interest.

> **Use any excess cash flow each month to pay down the highest interest rate debt first.** Whether your highest interest rate debt is your largest or smallest balance you should focus your payments on these debts because you are reducing the maximum amount of interest charged and therefore paying down your TOTAL debt amount more quickly.

> **Remember that some debt is tax deductible and some is not.** Interest on credit cards, automobiles and student loans are usually not tax deductible. Usually home mortgages and home equity loans are tax deductible. Consider the "after tax" cost of debt when comparing debt balances interest rates and always focus on the highest interest rate debt first.

> **Debt consolidation:** Consolidating high interest rate loans such as credit card balances into a home equity loan can be quite beneficial for several reasons. First, the interest rate is generally significantly less on home equity lines than credit card debts. Consequently, more of each payment goes towards paying down the principal rather than paying interest. Second, the interest paid on home mortgage debt may be tax deductible and thus the interest can reduce your federal and state income tax liability. This tax savings from home mortgage loans (usually in the form of a tax refund) can be used as an annual lump sum reduction in your debt balances thus accelerating your journey to debt freedom.

When using debt consolidation be careful not to rely on the transfer of debt as a mental crutch. In order to get the maximum benefit of using a debt consolidation approach, take the total amount you were paying on all of the loans consolidated and make one single payment to the debt consolidation balance. Because the interest rate is lower and the repayment time period may be longer, the minimum payment will be lower than what you were paying before. A lower payment may tempt you to fall into the trap of paying the lower amount: DON'T DO IT! Debt consolidation only works if you pay the same amount to the debt consolidation loan as you were paying on all of the previous debt payments. This action accelerates reducing your debt.

Think about what you will be able to do once you no longer have debt. Yes, zero debt. Give yourself a tangible reward so you mentally know that all of the hard work of getting out of debt will be worth it and begin today.

KEY TAKE-AWAYS:

> DEBT ELIMINATION IS A MARATHON

> BE STRATEGIC WHEN DEVELOPING A DEBT REDUCTION PLAN

> PAY OFF HIGHER INTEREST RATE DEBT FIRST REGARDLESS OF BALANCE

CHAPTER TEN

✴ CHANGING TIRES ✴

Preparing Yourself for Change

When I began Ironman training, I already had experience in both swimming and running competitively from childhood. Riding the bike was an entirely different story. Of course I had ridden a bike as a child, but racing on a bike was totally different. In the "old days," we didn't worry about flat tires or air cartridges because if we got a flat, we simply got off and walked the bike home for help in repairing the tire.

I was fortunate in those early training days to meet Isaac. Isaac had been bike racing for years and knew everything there was to know about bikes, including how to change a tire quickly and efficiently. Early on he tried to teach me about changing flats but I was more interested in getting out there to ride as fast as I could. I always knew that Isaac would be there to change my flat tire. Isaac was constantly on me to learn bike mechanical skills. Over and over he said, "in racing I could hope for the best but I needed to be prepared for the worst."

Not taking his advice, Isaac decided to teach me a lesson in bike mechanics. More importantly, Isaac taught me "Male Ego Management" on a group ride with him and five other female riders. On that day when I had a flat tire and I looked over at him to change it for me, he just smiled. As I fumbled around for tools and the replacement tube, I could feel my blood pressure rising and the embarrassment growing while surrounded by other riders who were clearly getting annoyed with the length of time that it was taking me to change the tire. After that day, I became the fastest tire changer of all my friends and would always be the first off my bike to help someone else change their tire. Most importantly, my emotional outlook on racing changed. I would be excited at the start of each race and hopeful for everything to go well. The change was that I would prepare for every possible challenge that could arise while racing.

Today when I begin any race, I know that I might get kicked in the face during the swim, have a bike flat along the way or may develop severe blisters on my feet during the run. When those events happen, I have a plan to overcome the obstacle and keep moving forward. After 22 Ironman races, I have the practical solution for most any problem that occurs on the course. These solutions keep me moving forward so that I can complete the race within the 17-hour time limit. Having the solution is key so that when the unexpected happens, I am emotionally prepared to handle the problem and not have my day ruined by a flat tire.

In the previous chapters, we discussed the benefits of being debt free in retirement. Now let's make sure that you are well prepared to tackle the second biggest fixed expense most people face when entering retirement: Housing Costs.

Look back at your spending plan today. How much money are you paying for housing, excluding the mortgage payment? Expenses such real estate property taxes, homeowner's insurance, utility bills, repairs and maintenance, lawn maintenance costs and other housekeeping expenses can amount to a very large number. Take a moment to complete the home expense worksheet below to see how much your home is really costing you.

HOME EXPENSES

HOA Dues

Home Owner's Insurance

Home Services

Home Supplies

Lawn & Garden Maintenance

Other Expenses

Real Estate Taxes

Repairs & Maintenance

Utilities (electric, gas, water)

GRAND TOTAL	$

For most people, where and how they live is directly related to their lives today. I hear from clients, "I live in this school district for my kids" or "I need this much house because I have three children." Makes perfect sense for today. Will it make sense in the future?

When we talk to clients about the future, we hear the same thing: "Change is hard!" Yes, change is emotionally hard especially when talking about moving from a home that you may have lived in 10, 20 or even 30 years. By being open to the possibility of moving and downsizing your current home to a smaller one, your monthly fixed expenses can be reduced. Downsizing may give you more flexibility with the money that will be going out during retirement. Benefits of downsizing your home are:

> **Mortgage reduction or payoff:** If you are too close to retirement to pay off your home during your working years, the sale and downsizing of your existing home may provide the ability to be debt free. By using the existing equity at the date of retirement, you could sell your current residence and use the net cash proceeds as your price ceiling on your retirement home.

> **Reducing real estate tax costs:** By downsizing, your annual real estate taxes will most likely be less given that real estate taxes are based upon the value of your

home. You may also reduce your real estate taxes by moving to a lower cost of living location. The millage rate (the real estate tax rate) may be lower in smaller towns than bigger cities.

> **Real estate school tax exemption:** Real estate taxes are usually made up of two taxes—one to run the local government and one for the local school operating budget. Some counties provide residents of retirement age an exemption for the school taxes portion of the real estate bill. Before you decide on the location of your next home in the downsizing process, check the county's rules regarding this exemption.

> **State income taxes:** Though not directly related to actual housing costs, where you live can affect the amount you pay in State Income Taxes. Florida, Texas, Wyoming, Nevada, Alaska, South Dakota and Washington State all have no state income tax. When planning for your future home, consider these states for a possible residence.

> **Home insurance costs:** In general, with a smaller house you will pay less in-home insurance costs.

> **Utility costs:** With a smaller house, you will usually pay less in heating and cooling bills. These bills go unnoticed until they begin to put a pinch into your cash flow.

> **Repairs and maintenance bills:** A smaller home generally, over time, will cost you less to repair and maintain. Roof replacements, yard maintenance and other upkeep can add up quickly for homeowners in retirement. Also consider the age of your next home purchase. The big costs of maintaining a home such as AC units, roof replacement and other major mechanical expenses related to older homes can put a big dent in your retirement cash flow. Buying a newer home will help reduce the possibility of this impacting your retirement.

With a plan to enter retirement with no debt and very low monthly fixed expenses, you will be more in control of your spending which will allow you to enjoy the ride but be ready just in case you get a flat along the way. Now that we are prepared for the journey, let's put some gas in the tank.

Key Take-Aways

> Change is hard

> Focus on the benefits that change brings

> Review home downsizing advantages

CHANGE IS ALWAYS
SCARY. THE FIRST
STEP IS SIMPLY THE
DECISION TO MAKE
THE CHANGE.

CHAPTER ELEVEN

My Bald Head

Inflation and the Impact on Your Money

Ironman triathletes, in general, can be Type-A personalities. We want to go, go, go. You would not describe us as those that go with the flow. Part of a successful triathlete's toolbox is trying to control as much of the training and the racing as possible. Everything from how we train to the food we eat has been tested, analyzed, and sometimes overdone. Every year after a race, I go on vacation and let my hair down. No schedules, no plans, just fun, food and relaxation.

After my race in 2016 I vacationed in Italy. The weather was perfect, the food phenomenal, and the countryside was beautiful. One evening, as I was drinking a glass of Brunello and watching the sun set over the Tuscan landscape, I thought, "I'm going to shave my head."

A week later, back at home, I looked in the mirror. Like most men, my hair has been thinning for 25 years. If I looked in a foggy mirror, with my head tilted one way and the light shining another way, I could convince myself I still had the hair I remembered in college. When I did start to notice my hair challenge, I was determined not to do the comb-over. "High and tight" is how I described my haircut. For 25 years, people assumed I had been in the military.

Coincidentally, the week I returned home was also the week of my scheduled haircut: every three weeks on Thursday with my stylist, Michael. I have been going to him every three weeks on Thursday for 25 years. Did I mention that triathletes were a tad bit Type-A? I walked in at 4:00 p.m. sharp and said, "Cut it as tight as you can because this is my last appointment. You aren't going to see me again."

Over the years I had threatened to shave my head during conversations with Michael, but this time I went home and did it. I thought I looked dramatically different. After a couple days, I loved it and I loved how it made me feel. The positive feeling that resulted was from finally being in control of the way I looked.

Whether gaining weight or losing hair, inflation happens so slowly that you hardly notice. How does inflation impact our retirement planning? In simple terms, inflation means that the price you pay for everything from the morning cup of coffee at Starbucks to the trip to the beach costs more over time.

For example, if a cup of Starbucks coffee costs $4.50 today, 10 years later it will cost $6.05 and 20 years later it will cost $8.13. The change in price of coffee from $4.50 to $8.13

may not seem like a lot but it is almost DOUBLE the cost to buy the same cup.

Some retirees comment on the fear of inflation. This fear often results from not being in control when it comes to the price increases that happen during the retirement years. Given that the average retirement lasts more than 20 years, the effects of Inflation are a real concern. To combat inflation, we must create a plan that addresses the impact of rising costs over time.

Simply put, to combat the impact of inflation while retired we must:

> Be debt free

> Have low fixed expenses

> Invest for the long term

I could not do anything about my hair loss, but I could take control of the way my head looked. You too can take control of your future income stream by acknowledging and planning for the effects of inflation over what hopefully will be a long retirement.

Key Take-Aways:

> Over time inflation eats away at your purchasing power

> Invest for the long term

CHAPTER TWELVE

✳ ORANGE TREES ✳

The Basics of Growing Your Money

I love oranges.

I love to peel them and I love to eat them. I love a tall, fresh squeezed glass of orange juice. Heck, I even use them in my morning smoothie sometimes.

Money is like an orange. Every day you can choose to eat your orange or save it. Once you eat the orange, it's gone. If you peel the orange, open it up and look inside, what do you find? Orange seeds. If you take the seeds, plant them in your back yard and water, fertilize and care for your seeds for the next 15 years, they become an orange grove. Once you have orange trees in your back yard you can go outside, pick an orange and have it for breakfast every morning. Even if you eat all of the oranges that your trees produce in one season they grow back and you can eat oranges next year as well.

Creating financial wealth with your money is as simple as oranges. Just like the orange you had for breakfast this morning, you have a choice every day with the money you spend. Are you going to spend all of it or are you going take a small amount of your money (seeds) and plant (invest) them for the long term?

I use the orange analogy to illustrate three very important challenges when it comes to accumulating wealth with one simple story. The first challenge people have in accumulating wealth is that they want to eat all of the oranges they have every day. They have to decide to put some of the seeds in the ground and make the decision not to eat. You get to decide. You choose whether to spend or to save every day. I am not suggesting that you should go hungry by any means. What I am saying is that by not spending all that you have every day, you will have a little money—or seeds—that you can begin to invest for your future.

The second challenge, waiting for the trees to grow, takes time and patience. It can take up to 15 years for the seeds to grow into mature, fruit producing trees. If you look outside your window every day, it appears that your trees are not growing. The growth is so slow it is easy to believe nothing is happening. I recommend taking a picture of your trees once every six months and comparing the old picture to the new picture in order to see your progress.

Sometimes, people believe that their trees are growing, but just not fast enough. They want to move their trees to a different patch of ground to get better soil. What they do not understand is that when you uproot a tree, you have to wait a period of time for the roots to get re-established so that the tree can start growing again. I see the same thing when it comes to people and their investing strategy. I say to clients all the time that your money will grow over time using almost any strategy as long as you stay consistent. You can make money in real estate, growth stocks, value stocks, bonds and many other investments. The only time you usually don't make money long-term is when you keep changing the strategy as the wind blows. By changing strategies, you will most likely be overpaying for your investments or spending excess costs with fees to keep making the changes.

The third challenge is when you get ready to retire, think of your investments like your orange trees. When you look outside your window, you will have an orange grove. You are not going to eat the trees but rather the fruit off the trees. Every season your trees will produce fruit, which you can eat. Some years the trees produce more fruit than other years, similarly in some years your investments will produce more income than in other years. Given that you have developed your financial plan with no debt and low fixed expenses, you will be better prepared when less income is produced in any given year.

Let's get started planting some seeds.

Key Take-Aways:

> You get to decide

> Stick with your investment plan long term

Money is like
an orange.
Every day you
can choose to
eat your orange
or save it.

CHAPTER THIRTEEN

✳ ARROW HELMETS ✳

The Best Way to Save

By now you know that triathletes can be a tad bit obsessed about some things. I am no different. A few years ago, I started searching for a new bike. The bike I was using was almost eight years old and after 10,000 miles, it needed an upgrade. I was riding a Cervelo P3. When I bought the bike, it was the most advanced Triathlon bike on the market. I loved the bike and went to my local bike shop to talk to them about a new one. I was told that Cervelo had come out with a new upgraded version of the bike called the P4 and they had all the great marketing slicks for my review. The bike looked awesome and not surprisingly came with an awesomely high price tag. Before I left the shop, I asked them if Cervelo was still making the P3 and they replied, yes.

As I began my research into the bike, I asked myself if the new version was worth the extra $3,000? I read all of the articles about yaw angles and wind tunnel testing, as they certainly made it seem like I would be a whole lot faster on the new bike. But, I wanted some real proof. After scouring the Internet and sending emails to Cervelo, I finally had my answer. The new bike would save me 14 seconds per 40 kilometers, which translated to saving less than two minutes time over the Ironman course. After sharing this information with the bike shop, they told me I could save more than 15 minutes on the course by spending a $100 on a new bike arrow helmet. Sometimes the simplest solutions can cost the least and give you the biggest bang for your buck.

The same thing can be said for saving money. When asked what the best way to save is, I always tell new clients that using a retirement plan to save money will give them the biggest bang emotionally and financially.

Conquering the emotional piece is key to saving. When I ask people why they are able to save so much money in a 401(k) or similar retirement plan, I get the same answer: "because I never see the money in my personal checking account." Using a 401(k) plan helps you with the emotional piece of saving because:

1. The money is taken out of your paycheck so it never hits your checking account. If the money never hits your checking account, it is less likely that you will spend it.

2. Because you are contributing regularly, you can start with a small amount each paycheck to help lessen the impact in your take home pay.

3. As you get raises it's easier to put a little more into the 401(k) plan each year because you were not accustomed to spending that money.

The 401(K) provides a lot of great financial benefits as well.

1. By using a 401(k) you put the money in "pre-tax" so you don't have to pay income taxes on the money you save until you take it out.

2. An Employer Match: Some employers will match some or all of your savings into the 401(K) plan thereby, turbo, charging your savings plan. I like to call this "free money"!

3. Dollar cost averaging: Just a fancy term that means you are consistently putting money into your investments, automatically buying more shares of investments when the market is down and buying fewer shares when the market is up. Dollar cost averaging also helps with the emotional part of saving as well. To buy when everyone, including the local expert, is telling you the sky is falling is hard, but by investing every time you get paid, you can put your retirement savings on autopilot.

Saving does not need to be scary or complicated. Saving can be as simple and cost effective as buying the arrow helmet!

Key Take-Aways:

> Retirement plans are the best way to save

> 401(k) plans take the emotions out of saving

SOMETIMES THE
SIMPLEST SOLUTIONS
CAN COST THE LEAST
AND GIVE YOU THE
BIGGEST BANG FOR
YOUR BUCK.

CHAPTER FOURTEEN

✳ SWIM PRACTICE ✳

Feeling Safe When Investing

The swim in an Ironman is 2.4 miles long. Most people finish the swim in somewhere between 1:00 and 1:45. The bike can take anywhere from 5:00 to 7:50 hours and the run anywhere from 3:30 to 6:00 hours. The swim is by far the shortest of the three disciplines. Ask most triathletes which event they fear the most, and the overwhelming majority will tell you it is the swim. The thought of swimming with 3,000 people all headed in the same direction at the same time can create panic.

In the past, I have had people swim over top of me, kick me in the chest so hard that I thought I could not breathe and had my goggles ripped off by someone taking their next stroke. Heading down to the swim start always puts my stomach in knots. It is the emotional stress of knowing something could go wrong. Horribly wrong.

I know how to swim and of the three events, it is my best; but to this day, I still spend three days a week at the pool.

Getting up at 4:30 to attend the Masters swim practice is not to learn how to swim or to stay in shape. For that I could get by with one day a week at this point. Why do I go? I go to be emotionally prepared for the swim. That's right, emotionally prepared. I want to know that if the bad thing happens, the kick to the face, the swim over or any other bad thing, that I am ready and I know that I will survive. I go to swim practice to "feel" safer in the water.

What do you do to feel safer when you are investing your money? The first thing we suggest when someone is getting ready to start investing, after they have learned the best way to save, is to make sure they have their emotional safety blanket ready. That blanket is your Cash Safety Net. Read any financial planning book and a recommendation is made to have 30, 60, 90 or 180 days-worth of cash on hand just in case you lose your job or an accident happens. The safety net is good for these reasons, but I would also suggest that the cash is your emotional security blanket.

That's right: your Cash Safety Net needs to be large enough to provide emotional support before and while you are investing. The Cash Safety Net is not designed to earn a rate of return that will help you obtain your financial goals. It is there to help keep you from making a bad decision. When the stock market goes down 20 or 25%, and it will, just knowing that you have a Cash Safety Net helps keep you from making an emotional decision to sell your investments out at the bottom, thereby losing a lot of money. Stated another way, cash allows you to be less fearful about your investing and financial planning. As we said earlier, the further you can keep your money from your emotions, the more money you will have.

KEY TAKE-AWAYS:

> EXAMINE YOUR EMOTIONS BEFORE INVESTING

> USE A CASH SAFETY NET AS AN EMOTIONAL BLANKET WHEN INVESTING

CHAPTER FIFTEEN

⚹ INVESTING 101 ⚹

The Fundamentals of Investing

Tinted or clear goggles? Thick or thin wetsuit? Tri or road bike? Gatorade or Powerade? There are so many choices that must be made when racing. Pretty soon the new athlete is overcome with the complexity of the decisions to be made when entering the sport.

The same is true when it comes to investing the money you have spent time, effort and energy earning. If we pull back the microscope, we find that your choices in investing really come down to three simple ideas:

> Invest your money in cash

> Invest your money like a lender

> Invest your money like an owner

Each of these options has pros and cons.

CASH:

Keeping your money in a cash account makes you "feel good". Why do I say this? When you put your money in cash, you don't have to worry about losing it. Cash does not fluctuate in value so every time you look at your account balance the money is still there. As you deposit more money into your cash account, your value grows. That makes us feel good.

The downside to cash is that your money is not making any money on itself. Said another way, your cash is not earning anything and so the only increase in your account comes from your hard work, not from your money working for you. As we discussed previously about my bald head, inflation is always eating away at the purchasing power of your money anywhere from 1-3% per year. After factoring in inflation, if you invest your money in cash, you are guaranteeing yourself a loss of purchasing power each year even though you may not realize it until it's too late.

LENDER VERSUS OWNER:

Investing your money in bonds (sometimes referred to as fixed income securities) is making the decision to lend your money to some company or government entity. Investing in stocks (sometimes referred to as equities) is making the decision to become a partial owner in a business. Let's look at an example:

You decide to buy a home. You purchase a $500,000 house and put down $100,000, or 20%, and you get a loan for the remaining 80% balance, or $400,000. You are the owner of the house and you have 20% equity in the property. The bank has loaned you money at a 3% interest rate for the purchase and they are the Lender.

Five years later you get a promotion requiring you to move to a different city. You accept an offer to sell your house for $600,000 after paying closing costs and fees. You go to closing and who gets paid first? Assuming you had an interest-only loan on your property and you had paid no principal during the five years, the bank gets paid back their $400,000 before you get paid anything. The bank is happy because they get the original amount that they loaned you plus the annual interest payment equal to 3% per year. How do you feel? Pretty good, right? You bought a home, put down $100,000 and five years later you sell the home and walk away with $200,000, a profit of $100,000, which equates to an annualized return of 14.29%. This is when it is both a good emotional and financial decision to be an owner.

To continue the example, you move to a new city where the cost of living is the same. You decide to buy a home for $500,000, putting down the $100,000 you had from the sale of your old home as your 20% equity and borrowing the remaining $400,000 or 80% from the bank. You are able to get another 3% interest only loan.

Unfortunately, five years later your company downsizes and you have to sell your home. If the real estate market is sluggish, you might accept an offer to sell your home for a net of $450,000 after commissions and fees. When you go to closing, who gets paid first out of the $450,000 proceeds? The bank gets paid $400,000. Is the bank happy? Yes. They get paid the full amount of the money they loaned you plus 3% interest per year. How are you doing? Well, not so good. You invested $100,000 into the home and you lost $50,000 when you had to sell. This example demonstrates the downside of being an equity investor, times when you are forced to sell when the market is down. By having a Cash Safety Net, no debt and low fixed expenses you are more in control of the timing of when to sell your ownership investments.

BONDS:

Bonds, or fixed income securities, provide a consistent cash income source in the form of monthly, quarterly or annual interest payments. The payment of the interest and the return of principal are considered safer because they have a liquidation preference of payment over the owners of the company (the equity holders). Just as the bank got paid first at both closings of the houses above, so does the bond holder get paid first if the company is liquidated.

The trade off when deciding to purchase bonds is that the interest rate paid on the bonds in most circumstances is lower than what an investor is expecting to earn when investing as an owner. Lower risk generally equals lower return over time.

Stocks:

When investing in stocks, you are investing as an owner. Your potential return is higher than investing as a lender (bonds), but you also have a greater potential of loss as in the case of the sale of the second home. As an owner, the value of your investments has more price volatility due to changes in the economy and, more importantly, changes in investor sentiment. This sentiment is the way they "feel" about the companies in which they are invested. Experts generally accept that investing in stocks will grow the value of your investments at a rate above inflation so that you are able to both take annual distributions at 3-4% and still grow the principal of your account, which protects you against the effects of inflation.

As we have been discussing throughout this book, the key to a successful retirement is having the ability to be flexible in weathering the ups and downs of your cash flow once you retire. Your portfolio must not only provide you with cash flow to live on in retirement, but be able to grow cash flow year over year as the costs of goods and services rise. By being debt free and having low required monthly expenses, you will be able to take less when the market is down and take more when the market is up.

It's a long race. The more you know about your money and the questions you should be asking your financial coach, the better off you will be. A good financial coach will want to spend the time with you to develop an investing plan that is right for you. This plan will not only balance the investment portfolio, but will also balance how much emotional volatility you can handle when it comes to your money.

KEY TAKE-AWAYS:

> KNOW YOUR OPTIONS BEFORE YOU INVEST

> DEVELOP YOUR INVESTING PLAN WITH A COACH

IT'S A LONG RACE.
THE MORE YOU
KNOW ABOUT YOUR
MONEY THE BETTER
OFF YOU WILL BE.

CHAPTER SIXTEEN

KONA: THE FINISH LINE

You Can Do This!

Your journey to financial freedom starts with one step: the decision to begin. My goal with this book was to provide a simple road map to help you with the process. Though the process is simple, it is not always easy. It takes courage to be disciplined and consistent along the way and to keep moving forward even when life throws you curve balls. By eliminating debt, lowering your fixed costs and investing for the long-term, you can control both your financial and emotional life.

If you choose to use a Financial Coach to help guide you, remember a few things. First, even though you have a Coach, you are still the decision maker. Educate yourself, as much as possible, with your Coach's playbook so that you know and agree with the plan set out by your Coach. You want a coach who is trustworthy. You want an engaged group of experts; a strategic team that is competent and worthy of influence. Second, when searching for a Coach ask a lot of questions so that you know it is a good fit. Professional questions including years of experience, professional degrees and certifications, number of clients, when he or she is planning on retiring, are they fiduciaries, financial planning and investment style and many others help you get a sense of how they operate. Don't be afraid to ask tough personal questions as well like, how do invest they invest their personal money, how are they compensated, are they financially free themselves to get a sense of the person you may be working with for many years. Our website at www.IRCWEALTH. com provides a comprehensive list of questions for you to reference. Lastly, when searching for a Coach, take your time. As the old saying goes, anything good is worth waiting for. There is no need to rush such an important decision.

My journey to the Ironman finish line in Kona began with the simplest of things; a photograph taken the year after my father had passed away. I remember sitting with him the week before he died as we watched his beloved Georgia Bulldogs football team for the last time. We talked about his life and his battle against cancer that would take his life at the early age of 62. He knew that he was at the end, yet he smiled, laughed and loved like a man who had the world at his feet and a lifetime still to live. His positive spirit resonated through me that day and continues each and every day that I live.

A year later, I took up Ironman to not only get my body back into shape, but to get my life back in shape as well. The inspiration came from watching the Ironman World Championship in Kona Hawaii. To race in Kona, you have to qualify for the race by placing in the top finishers in your age group. For more than 15 years, I raced to qualify in remembrance of my father. I came close several times but never quite had the race I needed to qualify. I sometimes got jealous of those athletes who came into the sport and quickly qualified through hard work and God-given talent. Nevertheless, I continued my quest.

As I began to see my dream of going to Kona slipping away, I began to feel down because I thought I was never going to get there. I remember crossing the finish line for my 18th Ironman, and I thought I was done with racing. One night while having dinner with a close friend whose wife had qualified and raced many times in Kona, I learned of the Legacy Program, a program that allows athletes who have completed at least 10 Ironman races the opportunity to race in Hawaii.

Do you feel that you are never going to be able to retire or be financially free? Credit card debt, mortgage debt, kid's college; the list goes on. Does it sometimes seem that other people are in the fast pass lane while you inch along in bumper-to-bumper traffic? In my 30-plus years of working in the financial industry with more than 40,000 client interactions, I know the power of persistence. I love Calvin Coolidge's quote:

> *"Nothing in the world can take the place of persistence. Talent will not; nothing is more common than unsuccessful men with talent. Genius will not; unrewarded genius is almost a proverb. Education will not; the work is full of educated derelicts. Persistence and determination alone are omnipotent. The slogan Press On! has solved and always will solve the problems of the human race."*

Recognize right up front that the path to financial freedom is a long one and it will be filled with ups and downs. By keeping things simple and focusing on small steps forward, you will eventually cross the finish line into a financially secure retirement. Remember, life is a journey and not a destination. Make sure you enjoy your current life: smile, laugh and love along the way. Know this: yes, yes you can!

And as for me, thanks Dad . . .

Aloha